THE TOPIC OF CANCER

By

STEPHEN COPSON

All proceeds going to Cancer Research and Cancer Charities.

PREFACE &
ACKNOWLEDGMENTS

I just couldn't get off to sleep. Tried watching TV, reading and all the usual tricks. I've lost count of how many hot sweats I've had, resulting in my insomnia. I try cooling down by walking around the garden before returning to bed.

I'm still awake and it's now 5am. I suddenly thought that it might be a good idea to capture some of my thoughts and experiences and write them down.

So I grabbed my iPad. I only wrote the first few lines before finally dropping off to sleep.

So the therapy of writing my experiences down proved a helpful effect.

*

My written experiences might just help other prostate cancer sufferers and prepare them for what's in store. I know everyone is different and their treatment may well differ from mine. However, I would have liked to have read someone else's account before going through this journey.

Being diagnosed with cancer is very scary, your whole perspective of life changes in a blink. I was probably lucky that although diagnosed with an aggressive form of cancer, it was still confined to the prostate and hadn't escaped. Although a serious subject, I have tried to capture an element of humour throughout. I apologise if it offends some but relates to my personal experience and how I have dealt with PC (prostate cancer).

Proceeds

I've had such brilliant treatment that I do want to give something back so all proceeds from this short story are going straight back to the organisations that have helped me and Cancer Research.

My grateful thanks to all the staff at the Urology Department at Blackpool Victoria, my two Cancer Nurses, my Oncologist and my GP. All the staff at the Rosemere Cancer Foundation and a special thanks to everyone on Linear Accelerator 6.

Thank you all for helping to save my life.

A little limerick –

There was a young fella called Bill

Who swallowed an atomic pill.

He found his sexual organ

In a street in Glamorgan

And his prostate up a tree in Brazil!

MY STORY

"Stephen, have you used your micro-enema yet, and has it worked?" asked the Radiographer's assistant.

With a straight face, I replied, "Yes, but for all the good it's done me I might as well shoved it up my bum!"

For a brief moment she actually thought I'd swallowed the enema instead, until she saw the grin on my face. We both laughed.

This was part of my first session of my radiotherapy treatment for prostate cancer so I was a little anxious of what was to come as I was booked in for thirty-seven treatments! Great – they are going to zap the hell out of it and hopefully get me cancer free.

From the start of my diagnosis I'd decided that a sense of humour was paramount to getting through this experience, so let me take you back several months.

*

Back in September 2015 my wife Sue and I had finally sold our house and moved into a smaller two-bed true bungalow; we needed to get rid of the stairs, also to downsize. We wanted to create a low-maintenance property so as not to be a slave to the home and garden and we could sod off somewhere to enjoy holidays and boating without having to worry about the place. This was also to be our last move for our retirement.

I've often wondered where the word 'bungalow' originated from. I suppose a house builder ran out of bricks and said, "Let's bung a low roof on it," or something like that.

Anyway, the bungalow we'd just bought was very traditional and our tastes are very contemporary. The result was a complete modification of the property both inside and out which took about six months to complete. We had builders for the big jobs and had great help from two friends as every room needed to be re-planned and modernised. I took an active role, working long hours for the period, fitting new kitchens, bathrooms, bedrooms, etc. I'm an impatient sort of person so I wanted it finished as soon as practical but not forsaking quality.

We had booked a couple of cruises and a short break prior to selling the house and moving. We would never consider cancelling them as we would probably need the rest.

The first was a well-deserved break for a Christmas cruise. Then in February we had a one-night stay at a hotel in Cheshire to have a reunion with two other couples that we'd met on a previous Christmas cruise on *Queen Elizabeth*. During that reunion, it emerged that one of the guys – David – had been diagnosed with prostate cancer and he shared his experiences and treatment details.

I remember asking David, "What were your symptoms?"

He replied, "Nothing really, can't explain. Just didn't feel my usual self but couldn't put my finger on it and say this or that was wrong with me."

That brief conversation could well have saved my life!

I didn't feel my usual self either but put it down to all the stress of moving, the pressure of getting all the work done on the bungalow, plus all the physical work I had done.

My mind still thinks I can do exactly the same as when I was in my twenties. Probably didn't give it a second thought and make any connections at that stage.

Another amazing, incredible fact is that out of the six of us at that reunion five of us have now had cancer diagnosed in the last two years – one bladder cancer, one bowel cancer, and three prostate cancers. We all joked it must be something in the Cunard food! But that's a separate story, suffice to say that cancer seems more rife than ever before.

*

It's now March 2016 and returning from our second cruise I decide it's probably time to book a GP appointment as despite having a holiday and a rest I did not feel 100%, but like David, couldn't say exactly what was wrong with me, just felt a little tired.

A couple of funnies –

On entering the surgery my doctor said, "Haven't see you for a while."

I said, "I know, I've been ill!"

He asked numerous questions about my health, including, "How's your sex life?"

I replied, "Infrequent."

My doctor said, "Is that one word or two?"

I then asked if he had anything for my liver and he gave me two pounds of onions!

*

Joking aside, and on a serious note, David's comments were obviously playing in my subconscious, so I said to my doctor, "Whilst I am here could you please check my prostate?"

I explained that I knew my body and felt that something wasn't quite right, although I could not expand further.

Most men, including me, wouldn't normally volunteer for such a procedure; it's the embarrassment of the rectal examination. I have this mental image and recurring dream of me screaming and running out of the surgery with my trousers around my ankles with my doctor attached via a rubber glove!!

Doctors are well accustomed to this examination and NO, you should not be embarrassed.

During my examination, I got a running commentary that yes, the prostate was slightly enlarged, but expected for someone of my age. It was smooth with no bumps or lumps and otherwise quite normal.

I remember thinking, *Wow, that's a relief.*

My doctor then said, "Just to be on the safe side I'll organise a blood test for you. Don't worry, you won't hear from me unless there is a problem, but if you want to you can ring up in about a week's time to check the results."

I felt reassured from his comments during the rectal examination.

I left the surgery feeling much more relaxed and that I'd probably overdone things rather than anything serious being wrong with me.

Then what a shock the next evening when the phone rang and it was my doctor.

He explained that the blood test had come back and my PSA level was higher than normal.

He explained that in many cases you live with prostate cancer as you will probably die of something completely different. Not a great opener for a conversation!

(PSA stands for Prostate Specific Antigen. Basically, the prostate is the only item in a man's body that produces this antigen. If the blood test reveals a higher than normal antigen level in the bloodstream, this can be an indication of prostate cancer.)

He continued. Many prostate cancers are quite docile and only regular monitoring takes place, but there are aggressive types that need a more radical approach. My PSA was only 5.26 whereas it should be around 4 for someone my age. PSA levels can go into the thousands so my results were only marginally over.

He also stated, "It could be an infection of the prostate, so we could give you a course of antibiotics for six weeks, then retest your PSA level. Or I can arrange for you to have biopsies taken at the hospital which can be arranged urgently."

I was now scared. The gravity of the situation was not sinking in, I didn't know what to do, whether to opt for the antibiotics or go straight for the biopsies. In a panic, I said to my doctor, "What would you do?"

The reply was no help, as my doctor apparently hates hospital procedures and said, "I am the wrong person to ask."

Initially I said, "Let's go for the antibiotics," but after putting the phone down realised that I would be living a nightmare for six weeks till I was retested. Would my nerves cope with that? What would happen if I wasted these six weeks and my PSA level was still high? Plus, if it was cancer I would be giving it six weeks to grow or possibly set up home somewhere else.

My mother, father, and sister had all died with cancer and secondaries were the main culprit.

So I rang back and opted for the biopsies. That was two days before Easter. I was fast-tracked and went for the biopsies the following Tuesday i.e. the day after Easter Monday.

Couldn't have had any quicker service.

I travelled to my local Blackpool Hospital Urology department for the biopsies. On that day I had to do a urine flow test.

First I must explain that my flow has not been brilliant for some years – I literally had two flows. It never went straight – one flow went slightly left and the other went slightly right! My wife nicknamed me Billy Two Rivers after a famous Red Indian wrestler in the 1970s. Because of this problem, in public toilets I never stood at a urinal, fearing I might splash the shoes of the two gentlemen in the adjacent urinals!

Plus, you can imagine the surprise if someone next to you saw two flows – they'd probably think you had two willies!

So basically, to pee I always sat down in the cubicle and opted never to use the urinals.

Being shown to the flow test room, I informed the nurse that I always sat down, so she told me to use the female contraption as she left the room. By this time I was absolutely bursting; I'd been told to arrive with a comfortable bladder, but the appointment was running an hour late so I was really full and desperate.

I dropped my trousers and sat down onto the toilet seat of the contraption, but didn't realise at this stage the receptacle to collect the fluid wasn't lined up!! Hence when I realised that I was filling up my trousers instead of the receptacle it was too late!

It was very embarrassing at the time but now makes me laugh when I recall the dilemma.

The moral of the story is also never to wear light-coloured trousers when attending hospital appointments.

So, with very damp trousers I was finally called in for the biopsies.

I won't lie to you, I found it very unpleasant. It's not so much painful, as I believe the inserted camera and mechanism that grabs the samples also gives you a shot of local anaesthetic.

Put it this way, I was glad when the final 12th sample was taken and the procedure was over.

The doctor and nurse performing the procedure were very kind and informative. They explained what was going to happen and were sympathetic to my care. They took the samples at a very quick speed in order to minimise my discomfort.

The doctor asked how I felt and I replied that I was relieved it was over. I thanked him for the speed in which the procedure was conducted but commented I felt that I'd just been raped! That comment I really regret – although being honest, it wasn't meant to offend and I don't think it did. However, I do regret making it.

They informed me that I would hear the outcome of the lab report in about a fortnight.

My rear was numb and a little sore as I left the hospital, it felt like I'd got a cricket ball stuck up my bottom!

A nursing friend sent me a text to enquire how I was. I replied, "I think I've just smuggled a biopsy camera out of the hospital! What can we get for it on eBay?" Sorry, my weird sense of humour again but you have to laugh, it helps to get you through the treatments.

I was forewarned that I might have difficulty peeing afterwards, plus I would see blood in my urine for some time. That definitely happened. There was also a chance of a urinary tract infection which did raise itself a couple of weeks later. Unfortunately, I couldn't get a prescription quickly enough from my doctors' surgery as they wanted to confirm with the lab the infection. As a result of the delay the infection travelled to my kidneys. Eventually when I got some antibiotics they weren't powerful enough. Fortunately, my consultant at the hospital stepped in and gave me something far stronger which cleared up the problem.

*

Now back to the biopsy results – I wasn't expecting to hear anything for approximately 14 days but the phone rang three days after having the biopsies. I remember it well, it was a Friday at 3pm – it was also April 1st, Fools' Day. The receptionist asked if I could come into the Urology department for Monday at 3pm.

I then knew it was going to be bad news. They wouldn't be contacting me so soon if there was nothing to worry about. I said it was unfair to leave me in suspense for three days over the weekend and, "As you obviously have the results, could I speak to one of the Cancer Nurses?"

A Cancer Nurse called Helen duly rang me back and said she had my results. She advised that three out of the twelve samples were found to be cancerous and that my Gleeson score was 8 which she explained was aggressive. I've always stressed through this saga, please don't hide anything – tell me the truth, good or bad news.

I didn't sleep the following three nights, and duly went to the hospital for my 3pm Monday appointment where I met Helen for the first time. She explained all the procedures and what would happen next. I would need a bone scan to see if the cancer had spread, then an MRI scan to check the rest of my body for secondaries. I explained that I hadn't got any blood relatives left, I'd lost them all to cancer and it was the secondaries that resulted in my mum and sister's deaths, plus my father had died a few years prior with lymphoma so she could see how worried I was.

Helen really fast-tracked me – the bone scan was organised for a couple of days' time.

She rang me the day after the bone scan to tell me unofficially that it was clear. Wow, that was the first relief and the first bit of good news.

It was explained that you couldn't have the MRI

scan till two weeks after the biopsies; that is because there will be bleeding from where the samples have been taken and the blood would mask details of the scan.

Duly, my MRI scan was conducted two weeks to the day after the biopsies. Helen had fast-tracked me again. Yet again, Helen rang me two days after to give me my unofficial result which was also clear. I certainly celebrated with a few glasses of wine that night. Well done Helen and grateful thanks for your understanding and care.

I must say that period of 14 days was the worst of all. Waiting for the results, you worry yourself sick. It's really stressful, you imagine all sorts of things especially with a history of cancer and secondaries in your immediate family.

My two Cancer Nurses could be contacted by phone if I was concerned about anything – both Helen and Melanie have been brilliant. Your first reaction is that you want your prostate removed, quite normal to want the tumour removed and out of your body. They gave me reassurance and details of how things would pan out with the various treatments including hormone therapy. They explained the possible side effects, lack of libido, erectile dysfunction, man boobs, an increase in weight, hot flushes and night sweats.

I met with my Oncologist specialist doctor and Mel two weeks after the last scan to discuss and agree my treatment. I was beginning to get worried that it was over three weeks since being diagnosed and I hadn't had even a tablet yet. That was soon rectified, I left the appointment with a month's supply of hormone tablets, plus a schedule for my GP to administer hormone injections.

Two weeks after starting the tablets I had my first hormone injection which would last a month. If there were no problems with the monthly injection the next one would last for three months. These injections prevent your body producing testosterone; apparently the cancerous cells can't flourish without testosterone.

The good part was that I wanted to get away on a boating holiday. I'd already now had my monthly injection, so I was able to get my three-month injection prescription from my GP and take it away with me, all I had to do was find a surgery whilst on holiday to administer the injection. That proved to be more difficult than I thought. I spent nearly all day on the phone, I rang every surgery and not one was willing to administer my injection. In the end

Whitehaven A&E did it for me, once they were faxed confirmation of the prescription and instructions from my home GP surgery.

This three-month injection would take me from the beginning of June and last to the beginning of September. These injections are administered into your stomach. I didn't fancy an injection in that part of my body, as I am needle phobic! I worried unnecessarily as it was nothing to get anxious about.

*

I was six weeks into the treatment, thinking, *This is easy, no really bad side effects so far,* although my manhood had started to shrink and didn't work as it used to. My flag seemed to work at half-mast rather than fully hoisted!

But who cares? I'm getting treatment and this is saving my life.

I then had this three-month hormone injection at Whitehaven. Wow! What a difference! Immediate hot flushes and night sweats – the most I've had in one day is 36. That was when we had the hottest day of the year in July. Total lack of libido, plus, it's rather alarming to see your dick shrink even further! Now, it never bothered me before, getting changed in a men's changing room, but now I would definitely think twice! I get this feeling that one day I'll wake up to just a pair of balls! Plus, my flag isn't even half-mast now, there's no breeze and it's definitely droopy!

That's the one thing they don't seem to tell you – your manhood will also shrink as the hormones do their job of shrinking your prostate. Plus, when radiotherapy starts it will probably shrink further!

This did worry me, but my Cancer Nurse Helen informed me that things do gradually go back to normal after you finish the hormone treatment, although it can take up to a year after you've ceased the treatment. I suppose it's bad enough them having to break the news that you have cancer, I'd have probably felt suicidal if they'd told me my manhood would also disappear at the same time!!

I had the thought to maybe take Viagra that my GP had prescribed, but with no sex drive you have no inclination to take the tablet. Plus, with my recent luck the tablet would probably get stuck in my throat and I'd end up with a stiff neck instead!

I have to make a joke about losing my sex drive. I start looking in cupboards and drawers or under the bed. My wife says, "What are you looking for?"

I say, "My libido, I've left it somewhere!"

If I'm out I pretend I've got a missing dog,

whistling then shouting, "Where are you, Libido? Here, Libido, good boy, come back to Daddy!"

Although a serious subject the humour helps to ease the problem. Plus, I enjoy making others around me laugh.

I also joke that when this is all over I look forward to going through puberty again!

*

I had a peculiar side effect that my vision went blurry in my right eye two days after I'd had this three-month injection. I went to the opticians and they rechecked my eyes and gave me a new prescription. Two days later I had to go back to my original prescriptions because I couldn't wear the new one and my sight had seemed to go back to my previous prescription. Very strange.

My optician also broke the news to me that I now had cataracts! This is very strange too, as I'd only had an eye test three months prior and there was no sign of cataracts then.

This has defied medical knowledge and is probably a coincidence, and may have nothing to do with the hormone injection.

Just after having my 3-month injection I also

noticed a small lump on my head. Probably a coincidence again; also, a black line appeared on one of my nails. I was hoping this wasn't nail cancer. You seem to get paranoid about any problems with your body or aches and pains, you think the worst and that it maybe cancer again.

I had a GP appointment pending and whilst there I mentioned these three odd things I was experiencing. My doctor told me that there was no explanation regarding my vision; it may have something to do with the hormone injection. The problem with my nail was nothing to worry about. However, the lump on my head was a slow-growing skin cancer. So, more bad news! So now I have two lots of cancer to get rid of! What a bummer!

My doctor advised to get the radiotherapy over with first of all, "Then I'll refer you to a Dermatologist." The skin cancer on my head was under a thick layer of hair, so not in direct contact with the sun.

I was always slim, but I have put on 12 pounds in weight. The hormone treatment does make you tired, plus the extra weight doesn't help. Six-pack has now gone and man boobs and a stomach are also appearing!

I can no longer fit into my trousers. I started with waist size 32 inch, progressed to size 34 inch and now just had to buy three pairs of 36 inch; the latter even have elastic waistbands!

The hot flushes are just a nuisance; you're dry one minute and soaking the next. You also tend to get woken up by them several times each night, disturbing your sleep and contributing to your tiredness. On the plus side the hormone treatment has sorted out my flow rate, I can now urinate with just one stream and with some pressure. Told my wife, "You'll just have to call me Billy One River in future!"

I normally always wore a jacket when I went out. You then have all the pockets for your wallet, mobile phone, keys, glasses, etc. However, wearing a jacket when you have umpteen hot flushes is no longer practical. So I invested in a man bag to hold all my bits and pieces, now I just wear a cotton T-shirt and that obviously helps keep your temperature down and makes the flushes less frequent and a little more bearable. Downside is that your mates take the Mickey out of you for having a handbag!

I must make a special mention to my GP. I affectionately call him Doctor Ted.

I have since heard that many doctors would have

just kept a watchful eye on my PSA level as it was so low at just 5.26, probably opting to re-check me again in several months' time. The statistics show that 76% of men with a raised PSA level don't have PC. I am extremely grateful to my Doctor Ted for being so vigilant. If I'd had a different doctor and been told to come back in a few months' time my aggressive PC could easily have spread to my bones or lymph glands and I could have been dealing with a much worse situation.

Thank you Doctor Ted, and have a great retirement. Your care, knowledge and wisdom will be sadly missed by Sue and me. You are certainly the best GP we've ever had.

Regrettably, the current PSA blood test is not accurate enough for indicating whether someone has an aggressive cancer, slow-growing cancer, benign tumour or no cancer at all.

This can result in some men having unnecessary biopsies when there is nothing wrong. About 2% of men with normal PSA levels have aggressive PC and this can go undetected. For these and other reasons there is currently no mass screening available.

I have read with great interest a new trial. This new STHLM3 test was trialled in a large group of over

58,000 men to see if it made any difference to diagnosing dangerous cancers earlier.

It proved to be far more reliable than the PSA test, but it also revealed the presence of potentially dangerous cancers that could easily be missed.

I look forward to the day when all men over a certain age can be screened.

There are over 11,000 deaths a year in the UK attributed to PC; it would be great if the new test could save many more lives.

I've no idea how long it will be, before or if the new test can be rolled out nationally. Presume it always revolves around cost.

*

My appointment to be mapped for the radiotherapy comes through. That's nothing to worry about, it's a CT scan. You use your micro-enema that you get from your GP on prescription and empty your bowels before the scan. They give you four little permanent dot tattoos which are used to line you up exactly for your future sessions. Don't worry about the tattoos, it doesn't really hurt, it's just a very light scratch. That was conducted at the Rosemere Centre at Preston Royal Hospital where I will be receiving all my radiotherapy sessions.

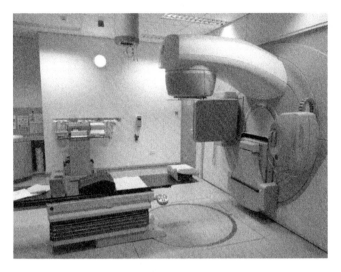

Linear Accelerator (LINAC) to administer radiotherapy.

*

It's now 21st July. I've just had my first radiotherapy session; staff are really pleasant and helpful, explaining what is going to happen, plus all the possible side effects. Radiotherapy is a painless procedure, which is great for a sissy like me! All my treatments are to be on Linear Accelerator number 6. They abbreviate this to LA 6.

After your micro-enema has worked, you have to drink two glasses of water and 20 minutes later you are in the treatment room. After you've been set up, the radiotherapy takes just a few minutes. I only have to take my micro-enema for the first five treatments. That's a relief as forcing myself to go, plus my normal motions, is making my bum sore!

The worst part so far is trying to get a parking space outside the centre!

So far so good. They tell you that you don't normally get any side effects for the first ten days. That's the first one done, only another 36 to go! I'll be here every weekday now for the next seven-plus weeks.

That night I was up and down to the loo seven times and thought my flow rate had reduced.

Will mention it to the staff before my next session.

Just had my second session, late afternoon, and it's Friday when I usually go out and meet our mates for a meal. So I need to get home as soon as possible. We normally always meet in a restaurant or pub. I have always liked a drink, but decided I was going to go on the wagon and give up alcohol whilst on radiotherapy and maybe for a month afterwards to give my body time to heal.

I am also now going to opt for caffeine-free drinks – so it's decaf tea and coffee and give up all fizzy drinks including Diet Coke. They don't want you to have fizzy drinks as this will increase gas in your bowel. I've already started drinking loads of still water to help keep me hydrated and give my cells the best chance of repairing themselves.

*

Whilst in the pub we had a great meal. My appetite is still good, but I also drank about four pints of water. When I went to the loo I had difficulty starting and my flow rate had reduced to a trickle. I can't believe I've got a side effect after only having two sessions. Don't want to be called Billy Trickle River by the missus! Must speak to the radiotherapy team on Monday to sort this out. I'm a little anxious that my flow has dropped so much that any more sessions may stop me urinating at all. My bladder will fill and then that will be an A&E job.

I start researching the problem and find that it's probably down to my prostate putting pressure on my urethra. I now nickname this my 'Franklin' after the Queen of Soul – Urethra Franklin! (Aretha Franklin)

The problem doesn't get any better over the weekend, I keep getting the feeling that my bladder is full and then when I try to go there is a delay, then the flow is decreased to just a trickle. It just resembles a dripping tap at times. I've now lost count at the of number of times I've had to go to the loo.

With my libido going AWOL, I was thinking that my manhood was only good enough for peeing – now even that has packed up on me!

The Weekend

Just to fill in some writing time, I must tell you the following. I never trusted pension funds but I always saved for my retirement, keeping the cash in savings accounts and latterly often invested the money in five-year bonds. Recently, a five-year bond matured.

Now I know common sense should prevail and I

should keep this money for its intended purpose!

When you have a scare, it certainly gives you a perspective on life and that every day is precious. So I'm thinking, my dick's shrunk, got no sex drive, so can't have sex at the moment, got to give up alcohol, I've put on 10lbs, I've lost my six-pack, getting man boobs, my trousers don't fit, can't go boating because of treatment schedule... What can I do to cheer myself up?

What's the point of keeping the money for a rainy day? I know, I'll buy myself a supercar.

So I decide on the BMW supercar – the i8.

We arrive at the dealership, I have the test drive, but Sue, my wife, declines the offer to accompany us. Basically, the deal is done and we both get in the car to drive home. If you don't know the i8, it has vertical-opening doors (not side-opening doors as on a conventional car). It also has very high sills to get your leg over when you want to get out. So to cut a long story short when we got home, poor Sue couldn't get out of the car!

I am gutted, because what's the point of having such a beautiful car that only one of us could use? I loved the car, but it had to go. That was really stressful. I was in mass panic for a week, wondering why I had bought it and how much money I was about to lose getting rid of it. Not what you really want when you are trying to cheer yourself up and remain stress free!!

To cut a long story short – luckily it developed a fault and the dealer had told us a couple of lies regarding the sale so that was all the pressure I needed to put onto the dealer to give us a full refund. We eventually got our money back.

Sue still wanted me to treat myself so we went straight off and bought a sports car that she could get in and out of. Finally decided on a Jag.

*

Here on my third radiotherapy session. Had a talk re my bladder experience with the radiotherapy team and apparently I drank too much water in quick succession on the Friday night.

I couldn't quite believe that I'd drunk too much water. I thought the whole idea was to drink at least two litres a day.

Things didn't improve over the next few days; it's difficult to remember how many toilet visits you've made so I started a spreadsheet! I've done some spreadsheets in my time for business, but never one entitled 'Peeing Record'! I recorded how much I drank of all liquids and how much I'd expelled. I was going for a pee 22-plus times a day! This can't be right! My 'Franklin' is really playing up!

The worst part was I was going up to eight times at night, so I was only getting a couple of hours' sleep. Plus, if I had a couple of hot flushes during the night my sleep was disturbed further. This was tiring me out. I've now had this problem for a week.

Anyway, I saw my Oncologist and he's now prescribed tablets to control my bladder. We had a little chat. I told him despite the side effects I was still perky and relying on my sense of humour to get me through everything. He asked if I had any other concerns.

I said I'd been looking on the US prostate cancer website and to combat your manhood shrinking and the lack of erections they had done some trials and recommended a small daily dosage of Viagra to bring things back to normal. Apparently. men were reporting that their dicks had grown back to the size and their erections had returned to the state they were before hormone therapy had commenced.

My Oncologist said he was aware of the trial and results, but said only to start this once I'd finished the radiotherapy sessions. About a third of a tablet per day.

I asked if it would be a slow or quick recovery to bring the erections back as I didn't want a surprise and suddenly pole vault out of the window!!

By his smile I think he saw the funny side.

Changing the subject, I was amazed at the Linear Accelerator (LINAC) machine that delivers your radiotherapy. At this centre the LINAC does a Cone Beam CT scan of the treatment area every single time before it delivers your dose of radiation to ensure accuracy and to ensure no problems. It's different to any other type of scanner whereby you lie down and the arms of the machine rotate around you.

During my first treatment I asked the radiographer, "How many patients do you treat from this one machine?"

She replied, "Forty a day."

So that's 200 a week and there are seven machines at this centre, so that's up to 1,400 sessions a week.

I also asked the cost and she replied, "When I was doing my training the cost was around £1m but now they have gone up considerably."

A recent check on Google had machines around 4 million US dollars – around £3m sterling. Thank heavens for our NHS.

At the end of every session I always say to the Team, "Many thanks for helping to save my life."

*

I've now been taking the tablets for three days to control my bladder and can report a decent night's sleep at last. Only up twice in the night and probably had a good six hours' sleep. I am now going to the loo about 12 times a day rather than 22! Hoping things will improve further as more tablets get into my system. My bowel movements are now watery due to the treatment and causing me to have a sore bottom, but the Team have given me a prescription to help.

*

So, now off for my eighth session and Sue has come with me for company.

After we leave, Sue suggests we stop off in Blackpool to do some shopping.

We park the car and head for town. On the way back as we pass Gypsy Petulengo's kiosk I casually glance across and she looks directly at me and beckons me across with a mysterious hand gesture.

We start up a conversation and I inform her that I last visited her 36 years ago when I was a single young man. She tells me that she is now 84 years old – she looks terrific for her age.

I always remember her telling me back then that I wouldn't find happiness till I lived in a house on a hill between trees. That turned out to be true.

So I didn't need much persuading when she asked if I would like a reading again. I opted for my palms to be read rather than the crystal ball.

I purposely wasn't going to confirm or deny anything till she finished her prophesies. I waited till she had finished.

Out of all the things she said that rang true – two things were a little uncanny and really stood out.

The first was that I was going to write a book! She certainly got that right! Here it is. I know it's more like a short story than a book, but she was spot on with that prediction. It's also not as if I'm an author, it's the first thing I've ever written apart from the 100 or so instruction books for domestic appliances that I wrote for my employment. However, nobody tends to read those!

She said the book was going to be a success. I explained that news made me very happy as all profits generated would be going to cancer charities including Cancer Research.

The second was that I'd got a very long life line and good health would follow me for many years to come. She kept saying, "You will not die from this." This current situation was just a blip and I would beat the cancer.

I left Gypsy Petulengo's feeling a lot happier. It wasn't planned to go there, it was purely by accident; plus, she'd boosted my confidence that I would beat this, and she wants a copy of the book when it's finished! I'm normally very sceptical, but this was weird.

*

Having my tenth radiotherapy session today. They

say any side effects usually raise their head after ten treatments. So here's to keeping my fingers crossed for the future. Whilst in the waiting area I strike up a conversation with a gentleman who is having the last of his 37 treatments today. I was pleased to hear he hadn't had a single side effect. Lucky person!

*

I've had a few more sessions and nothing to report. The tamsulosin tablets to control my bladder seem to be working.

*

Another strange happening has occurred. The peculiar lump on my head that was diagnosed as skin cancer has totally disappeared. I can't believe it; I've had no treatment. This is marvellous news. I contact my GP and ask him if he needs to re-exam the area and get confirmation that it's gone. I ask if the hormone treatment has anything to do with its disappearance. He says no and that the immune system is a fabulous thing. So, thank you immune system, that's one thing I no longer have to worry about.

Raises another question though! Why didn't my immune system destroy my prostate cancer? It needs a rollicking! I'll have to give it a good talking to! Probably too big a job for it!

*

Now onto my fifteenth session. My bladder problem has re-occurred, causing disturbed sleep again. Although it improved for a while I'm back to getting up between 4-10 times during the night. I'll mention it at my review tomorrow.

I am now planning what to look forward to, when my radiotherapy finishes. I will probably need a rest for a month, then I can book some holiday time.

So I'm already looking at where I would like to go.

It's very important through this process to focus on goals and to treat yourself, that way you stay positive and it's got to help your recovery. Plus, remember to laugh, even if it's laughing at yourself, because laughing is one of life's best healers. Finally, always try to remain positive and avoid the stress.

Some people with cancer often want to keep their diagnosis a little secretive or are reluctant to talk about it with others. I am the opposite and will gladly share my information with all. Keeping things bottled up doesn't work for me; sharing my experience and talking about it with friends has undoubtedly helped me and brought us laughter many times.

*

Now reached the halfway point – my eighteenth session today. Still struggling with both the waterworks and my bottom.

Things are falling into a pattern now. After two days' rest at the weekend from radiotherapy my side effects begin to get better. By Monday morning I can pee again nearly properly – but slowly through Monday-Friday things get progressively worse.

So I'm sat here waiting for my session and thinking about my sore bum when I suddenly have a chuckle as it reminds me of a funny.

*

A chap goes to the doctor regarding his bowel movements and informs the doctor that every time he goes it comes out like chips!

The doctor examines the patient, asks him to stand up and his bowel movement is normal, then asks him to sit down and it comes out like chips.

The doctor then leaves the room and returns carrying a huge scalpel.

The patient, very worried, says, "You're not going to operate now, are you, Doctor?"

Doctor replies, "No, I'm just going to cut six inches off your string vest."

*

Here again for my radiotherapy. Nearly every time I arrive and walk from the car park to the Rosemere Cancer Entrance, there is always someone smoking outside the entrance despite the No Smoking signs. There are dog ends all on the floor.

Just amazes me that patients have the audacity to smoke when they are being treated for cancer. If it's visitors, they should have more respect – just can't comprehend that people can do this.

I reckon they should be fined severely and the proceeds shared amongst all the Rosemere staff and Radiographers.

Fagging it – outside the centre.

I have remained very positive throughout my treatment. I had a relapse yesterday and for the first time felt a little depressed. This was due to me having a bowel mishap. The strange part about it was that I didn't know it had even happened.

I told my radiotherapists about it, stating that I'd tolerated all the side effects but this one really got to me, hence I was feeling down about it.

Apparently it's quite a normal side effect of the treatment.

I joked that the last time I shat myself was when I was three years old!

The man bag comes in handy for carrying a spare pair of emergency Y-fronts, wet wipes and a plastic bag! I knew it had multiple uses! The philosophy is that if you've got the tools to deal with an emergency you won't need it!

Still not sleeping very well, up numerous times during the night. About 2am I had the sudden thought – is there a collective noun for a group of radiographers? So the iPad came out and I Googled it.

To my surprise there were a couple of answers – the best was 'A Radiance of Radiographers'! I thought that was very relevant, can't wait to tell them on LA 6.

It's amazing the things you think of when you can't sleep.

Will wait till Friday when I have my review and see if I can get any alternative medicine for my waterworks as the tamsulosin isn't working 100% and I would love a proper night's sleep. I haven't mentioned it before but it's slightly painful when passing water. Plus, as soon as you've been you still want to go again, getting the feeling you don't quite empty your bladder every time. It's a really frustrating experience.

I must give you gentlemen diagnosed with PC a warning too. Probably, like me, you have been trained (more than likely by your other half) to always close the toilet lid after you have been.

I will try and put this next bit as politely as possible. Before radiotherapy everything solid that was expelled from my body always sank. Since the start of radiotherapy things have become much more buoyant!

I think they are commonly called 'floaters'.

You flush the loo, have a peep to see if everything has disappeared, then close the lid.

Regrettably, this is not enough! You need to go back and have a second peep!

These blighters have the ability to travel back around the U-bend and reappear! Not a great sight for the next person using the loo!

Just a warning for you all to be aware of.

I haven't been able to establish if this is a common side effect of radiotherapy or just confined to me. I really can't ask the other guys having treatment if they now have floaters! It wouldn't be polite or really ethical!

To combat the problem of watery motions and control my digestive and bowel system, I have needed to slowly change my diet.

No longer am I eating ten-plus fruit and vegetables a day, probably five now. Plus, I've had to ditch the Weetabix and wholemeal bread. I am now eating white bread. Whereby I'd have fruit after a meal – this is now biscuits or cake. So my healthy diet is becoming far less healthy. This is as recommended by the Team to stave off the diarrhoea.

They have also prescribed Fibrogel sachets to increase the fibre in my diet.

These are highly concentrated orange drinks. They smell really orangey when you add the water and mix them before drinking.

Now here's the funny side.

My wife keeps saying, "Can you smell oranges?" at various times around the house.

I haven't let on yet, but it coincides with every time I've passed wind!

*

I'm now up to my 27th radiotherapy session. It's a Friday so I will be having my review. Nothing really to report, although I am now getting the fatigue associated with radiotherapy. It's August bank holiday weekend so that's three days without radiotherapy – it will be a break for me, three days to recuperate.

During every radiotherapy session, the Team have to place you in an identical position lining up each of your four tattoo dots. There can be up to four Team members looking after you, mostly female. You have to pull up your shirt to reveal the dot which is at the top of your breastbone. You also have a tattoo dot on each hip which have to be lined up. There are green laser beams to assist the Team in getting everything precise. You also have to pull down your underpants to reveal the fourth dot which is just above your manhood.

To save any embarrassment they simultaneously cover this area with a square sheet of paper towelling from a roll. So you are now lying there with nothing visible.

This is fine till one of them walks past too quickly, creates a draught, and the paper disappears!

It's only happened twice. I'm not bothered anymore – you tend to lose your inhibitions; they must accidentally see plenty of men's bits. Plus, with the shrinkage, there isn't much to look at!

*

The week after the bank holiday is a short week, only four sessions. It's Friday again and another review. I've suffered this week with diarrhoea and passing water has been a real problem, especially at night. It's also been painful to urinate and I've had great difficulty starting. Never mind, only six more sessions to go and then I can start the road of recovery.

The problem with the diarrhoea is you don't get much of a warning.

I'd probably say you have 20 seconds from realising something is happening to getting to the toilet and dropping your trousers. So far I haven't messed myself. Trying to keep a clean record of only shitting myself once since I was three.

I'm hoping that my waterworks will hold out to the end of my treatment, the alternative of having a catheter fitted doesn't appeal – in fact after the shrinkage I don't think they'll find a tube with a small enough diameter!

With regard to the rear end I also don't fancy wearing Tena pants either!

*

I always arrive an hour early for my appointments to allow ample time to get parked. Today was a nightmare. The MRI scanner unit was parked up which takes over 40% of the car parking spaces available. I waited 40 minutes to get a space, then four cars including me shared the space of three bays to enable parking.

I didn't realise until later that two of the radiotherapy machines were broken, so patients were delayed and weren't coming out to drive home, so no spaces were being released.

The outcome was I had been given a parking ticket. Really pees you off!

The hospital farm out the policing of the car parks to a private company called Indigo.

I've tried to appeal but every time I try, they block

it and change their rules, making it as difficult as possible for you. They ask you to email; when you do this, they change the rules and say you have to appeal via their website. When you do this, you can't get more than a couple of lines of text into the box provided so it doesn't have all the information contained in your original email. Then you can't amend it and you've got about 5% of your appeal.

They obviously hope you will give up because it's so much trouble and that you will pay up. So annoyed I've now written to the MD of the parking company.

I know it's only £40 but it's the principal of the matter, when it's not really your fault. I've told him I refuse to pay but will gladly donate the same amount to Cancer Research or the Rosemere Cancer Centre. See if he's got a heart and if he agrees?

I've now spent three hours on this. I can't be the only one being fined. It's not fair to persecute cancer patients like this when the parking arrangements aren't fit for purpose.

I could do without the aggravation, especially when I'm so tired due to the treatment.

*

I've noticed over the past few weeks how breathless I've become. The Team at Rosemere say it is nothing to do with the radiotherapy or any of the medicines they have prescribed so I'm off to my GP to see what's causing it. My normal GP is on holiday and I see a new doctor. He advises my blood pressure is extremely low and they suspect that I might have a clot on the lungs. It's a possibility with prostate cancer. They give me a blood-thinning injection and tell me to get to A&E Blackpool ASAP.

Sat in A&E now waiting to be seen, just hope they don't want to keep me in.

They've now taken bloods, an ECG and chest X-ray. I've had my blood pressure taken numerous times and it's been normal.

Been here seven and a half hours now and still haven't seen a doctor yet. Sister now informs me that I'm going to be admitted, just waiting for a bed in the Acute Medical Unit.

*

I've only got four more radiotherapy sessions to do. I'm in Blackpool Hospital and I need to be in Preston Hospital for my 10.15am appointment tomorrow. Wonder what will happen? It's now 3am – still in A&E and have been informed that there are no beds available in the Acute Medical Unit; doubtful if I'll see a doctor now before morning. It's impossible to sleep here, too much noise going on. Plus, I'm up to the loo every 30 minutes or so. Just what you need when you are already tired.

This is Blackpool A&E midweek and it's surprising what you see; it's a real education. The police bringing in patients in handcuffs, or maybe they are taking them away for causing trouble – drug addicts, drunks, etc. What a huge change in society during my lifetime, we used to have respect. I feel so sorry for the staff who have to deal with it all.

*

It's now morning. I manage to get a message to my Cancer Nurse in Urology to tell her I've been admitted with suspected pulmonary embolism so she in turn can advise my Oncologist.

It's 10am and the doctor has finally been. He apologises for the huge wait (17 hours) and states they have been dealing with patients with life-threatening symptoms and they have to prioritise.

They won't let me out for my trip for radiotherapy until they have discounted anything seriously wrong with me.

Apparently my ECG was clear, my bloods are all clear – no infections.

Nothing visible on the X-ray. So I'm a mystery at present to find out what's causing the breathlessness under exertion.

The doctor is referring my case to the consultant to see if he requires a CT scan of my chest. So none the wiser at the moment with a diagnosis. Consultant arrives and he doesn't need a CT scan, so I can be discharged.

I've now missed my radiotherapy appointment and it can't be rearranged for later in the day. So an extra appointment will have to be tagged onto the end.

Instead of finishing on September 12th my last session now will be the 13th.

After my fair share of side effects and hospitalisation, good job I'm not superstitious!

The common consensus is that the breathlessness has been a side effect of the hormone therapy and not helped by the extra weight I am carrying around.

*

It's nice to be home and out of hospital. I hear my wife Sue calling me from a distance, sounds like she calls, "Hey, Stud." When I get nearer and hear it again I realise she's called, "Hey Stump!!"

Her nicknames for me are really creative and do

make me laugh. The information will be shared; it won't be long before all our mates start calling me The Stump as well!! I will just laugh it off! Just you wait till things return to normal.

I'm just wondering whether to write this book under a pseudonym and remain anonymous or not. Quite a few people know me locally – I don't really want people shouting, "Hiya Stump!" as I walk down the street!

*

Thursday's radiotherapy goes without a hitch. They are pleased to see me back and I have a review re my hospital admission. Thirty-four down, only three more sessions to go.

*

Well it's Friday and I have my review with my Oncologist today. Only two more sessions to go. This will be my last review before finishing radiotherapy. My next consultation will be in six weeks' time. Hopefully I will get an indication that the therapy has worked then. My Oncologist explains we will be looking for a PSA level of 1 or less.

We discuss my side effects after having the three-month hormone therapy injection and it's decided that my injection which is due to be administered later today should be a one-month injection instead. If the side effects are still apparent in a month's time, then I will then go onto tablets which will have less side effects, especially towards weight gain, sexual dysfunction, hot flushes, etc.

My Oncologist explains that my waterworks side effect problem which now has a name – Radiation Cystitis, can continue for several weeks after treatment has concluded.

It is also explained to me that when my radiotherapy has finished the treatment continues to work for a period, peaking about two weeks after your last session. All the side effects can continue for 4-6 weeks, hopefully things should have improved by the time I next see my Oncologist in six weeks.

*

Been serious for too long now, so here's another doctor funny.

Patient goes to the doctors, saying, "I can't stop singing 'The Green Green Grass of Home.'"

Doctor says, "You've got Tom Jones Syndrome."

Patient says, "Is it rare?"

Doctor says, "It's not unusual."

*

It's September 13th and my last session. I brought boxes of chocolates and a personalised thank you card for the Radiographers and Team on LA6. I am so grateful for their care.

You tend to lose several hours a day going for radiotherapy. Today, for my last session, I left home at 2pm. Unfortunately the appointments are running an hour late so with the rush hour traffic I will be lucky to get home by 6pm.

I generally lose 3-4 hours out of my day. Most of my appointments have been around 10am, so I can now look forward to a lie in for the next few weeks.

Another thing I must tell you. All through my treatment friends have come up to me and said, "Wow, you look really well." I don't know what they expected; probably they associate people with cancer looking grey with hair loss and weight loss. Although on the inside I have felt extremely fatigued, on the outside I have gained weight and my face has a glow, all probably down to the hormone therapy. It's also quite comforting that your mates keep telling you how well you look although you may feel absolutely knackered on the inside.

*

It's now a few days after I've finished my sessions

and I have developed some soreness to the skin in my groin area. Right at the top of each leg in the skin fold area. It's in the area where even walking is going to aggravate the soreness. You are warned that your skin might get tender, itchy or sore right at the beginning of your treatment. I had sailed through the 37 sessions and my skin had not been affected till now. Left unattended and it looked like the skin would break and start to bleed.

Just shows that the radiation continues to work well after your last session. I contacted LA6 re the problem and the Team told me to apply E45 cream, I've done that for only one day so far and already there is an improvement.

However, the next day I noticed the skin had broken, so I had to stop using the E45 cream and use a product called Hydrogel instead.

I just need to be right for the weekend as I'm going to celebrate my birthday in style and now have a few drinks. As I've been on the wagon for the past two months I'm going to take it easy with a couple of beers or wine, no spirits as this could aggravate my bladder. I've booked a Blackpool Cabaret Comedian Show with evening meal for ourselves and four friends. Still important to have something to look forward to and always to stay positive.

*

The day after my birthday and I'm pleased to report that the broken skin in my groin area has nearly totally healed. That's a relief as it was getting painful even to walk.

The six-week wait to find out if the treatment has worked is going to play on your mind. Nothing you can do really, but wait. No good worrying, I just keep thinking that these horrid cancer cells have been zapped on 37 occasions, how could they possibly survive? They must be all dead by now!

I liken the situation in my mind to a real war.

Our British troops have been fighting the cancer cells (by this I mean my immune system has), then we've needed some help from our Allies the Americans (by this I mean the radiotherapy). Now regrettably, when the Americans get involved in any war they tend to kill us by accident – they call it 'Friendly Fire'.

The outcome of the 'Friendly Fire' is that some of your good cells are accidentally zapped by the Americans. These good cells are in the prostate, bladder and bowel.

Now this is where the fantasy comes in – in a real war the good guys die and stay dead, but all my good guy cells will rebuild themselves! The dead cancer cells stay dead and become scar tissue.

Take that, cancer!

*

Well, a week has gone by since my radiotherapy finished. The main side effect still troubling me is the waterworks. Still painful passing water and going umpteen times, especially at night. The symptoms will hopefully get better as time goes on.

One bit of good news arrived today – my parking fine has been scrapped, so true to my word the £40 has been sent off instead as a donation to the Rosemere Cancer Foundation.

There's one thing that I haven't touched on, and that is the psychological effect on a man when he suddenly loses his libido and his body image. You feel that your masculinity has been seriously compromised.

I have certainly put on weight, around a stone now, and wouldn't rush to take my T-shirt off and sunbathe.

The lack of sex drive can be devastating too. I feel that I've been taken to the vets and neutered!! I now feel sorry for the dogs and cats I've owned!

Thankfully I have a very understanding wife. Sue has been very supportive, and at some stage in one's marriage love has to be more important than the sex.

You are both grateful that this treatment is hopefully going to cure you.

You also have to keep in your mind that this is a temporary side effect and your libido and body should return to normal when you come off the hormone treatment.

Although, I personally could be on the treatment between 2-3 years.

If I was married to a nymphomaniac, things could be totally different!

However, there is plenty of help from your support network to help you cope should you require it.

*

My wife Sue has read through my story so far and as a result a couple of the funnies have been edited out as she said they were a little rude and could have caused offence, which is the last thing I wanted to do. I did fight to keep them in.

You are now reading the edited version. She tells me I must be more like Bradley Walsh and not like

Keith Lemon! Fair point, but I don't take criticism lightly.

I have got my own back by saying I'm putting before and after pictures of my willy in the book! Only joking!

*

It's now three weeks since I went back onto a monthly hormone injection and I am pleased to report my hot flushes and night sweats have nearly disappeared, just the occasional one happens now. That previous three-month hormone injection just didn't agree with me.

So let's recap. I have had more than my fair share of the side effects since having the hormone therapy and radiotherapy, although on numerous occasions I have spoken to other patients who say they have had no side effects at all!

The luck of the draw, I suppose.

*

I've decided to list the **good** things and the **not so good** things associated with my personal treatment since being diagnosed. Let's start with the –

Not so good

The biopsies, the news you've got PC, waiting for the test results, putting on weight, man boobs, trousers don't fit, hot flushes, night sweats, sex drive disappears, willy shrinks, erectile dysfunction, urinary tract infection, difficulty peeing, painful when peeing, sleep deprivation due to numerous toilet visits, fatigue, diarrhoea, messing yourself, being hospitalised, tender or sore skin in the groin, a parking ticket and a car your wife can't get out of!

The good

I'm alive and my farts smell like oranges!

*

Men are notorious at turning a blind eye to health issues. I would urge all men to visit their doctor should they have any of the following symptoms. Wives and partners, too, should ask the man in their lives if he has any of these symptoms and if so make an appointment for him. Better safe than sorry, plus many of these symptoms don't necessarily mean you have cancer.

Urinary problems – weak urine stream, difficulty initiating urination, stopping and starting during urination; urinating frequently, especially at night; pain or burning with urination. These symptoms are also often associated with noncancerous enlargement of the prostate.

Blood – in the urine and semen.

Pain – in the hips, pelvis, spine or upper legs.

Pain or discomfort – during ejaculation.

Any of the above symptoms, please don't hesitate and don't delay – get to your doctor ASAP. It could well save your life. Far better to be treated early.

Well finally the six weeks have now passed since my radiotherapy finished. It's been a long wait. Most of the side effects have lessened. The breathlessness is still my main concern.

*

It's now the 27th October and also the date of my appointment with my Oncologist. I'm now off to the hospital to see him and to get the results for my PSA blood test that was taken two days ago. My fingers are crossed as well as everything else.

Hurray! Hurray! Yippee! Yippee! Yes! Yes! Yes! Yes!

My PSA is now expressed as a minuscule fraction! I have just been told by my Oncologist that I am now officially in remission (not cured – in remission).

You need to be in remission for five years before you are given the all-clear. I will be checked again in three months' time, then it will eventually go to six months, then yearly checks.

You can't begin to realise how grateful and how happy I am – 2016 has been a bit of a bummer year to say the least – this is the best news yet.

My Oncologist suspects that my breathlessness is down to the hormone injections so he is now swapping me onto a daily hormone tablet that will be kinder on the side effects and may offset this breathing problem.

He explains that it also causes less side effects associated with erectile dysfunction. So even better news all round! The Stump nickname will have to go! Take note, Mrs Wife!

The only downside is that I may get sore breasts!! It's a no-brainer really – a functioning willy and tender tits!

I will also need to continue taking the tamsulosin for the foreseeable future to control normal peeing functions.

*

I've not hidden anything during my journey and if you are also a PC patient I wish you all the best luck in the world dealing with this disease. Keep smiling throughout and keep a hugely positive attitude.

So with all my good news, it's now an ideal time to finish my short story. I always wanted to be able to finish it on a high, positive note.

I'll try to bring out updated editions over the next 4-5 years to let you know how I am progressing and more importantly, with all your help, the monetary figures we've raised for the charities.

The book will be available as a physical and an electronic version – available on Kindle also via Amazon.

*

I hope you've enjoyed my short book regardless of whether you are a PC patient or just an interested reader. I hope I have made you laugh at times. Cancer now affects one in two of us during our lifetime. When I was growing up I remember it being just one in six.

All I would ask is that if you have enjoyed my story please tell as many people as possible and ask them to buy it. I would ask that you don't lend the book out, get them to buy their own copy! More dosh for charity!

Put your comments on social media and try to get as much interest, please. My dream is it to be a best seller! Because – every penny raised will go to cancer charities including Cancer Research. Hopefully, one day in my lifetime there will be a cure for all cancers.

Love to you all,

Stephen (alias The Stump)

P.S. It's definitely now recovering!!